1

OUR WORLD

SECOND EDITION • WORKBOOK

Series Editors
Joan Kang Shin
JoAnn (Jodi) Crandall

NATIONAL GEOGRAPHIC
LEARNING

Australia • Brazil • Mexico • Singapore • United Kingdom • United States

OUR WORLD 1

SECOND EDITION • WORKBOOK

Unit 0

Welcome to Our World!

1 **Listen.** Read. Write. Use words from the box. TR: 0.2

Hi	name	seven	six

1. Hello. I'm Eddie.

   What's your ________________?

2. ________________. My name's Polly.

3. I'm ________________. How old are you, Eddie?

4. I'm ________________. It's my birthday!

2 **Read.** Write.

A _____ C D _____ F G _____

I _____ K L M _____ O _____

Q R S _____ U V W _____ Y _____

3 **Look.** Listen and circle. **TR: 0.3**

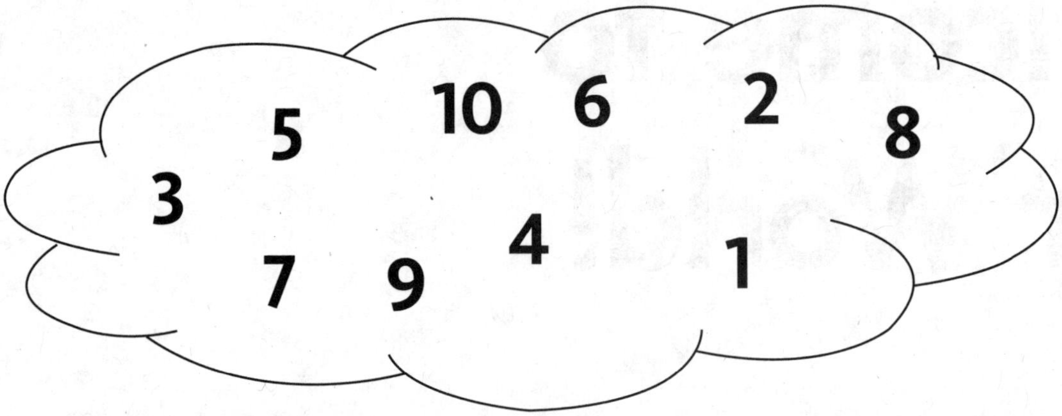

4 **Listen and read.** Look. Draw a line to match. **TR: 0.4**

1. a star
2. a square
3. a rectangle
4. a triangle
5. a circle

5 **Read.** Look at Activity 4. Color.

1. Color the square purple.
2. Color the circle red.
3. Color the rectangle white.
4. Color the triangle green.
5. Color the star orange.

6 Read and draw.

1. Draw three yellow stars.
2. Draw two black circles.
3. Draw one blue square.

7 Look and match. Write the number.

1. 

2. 

3. 

4. 

5. 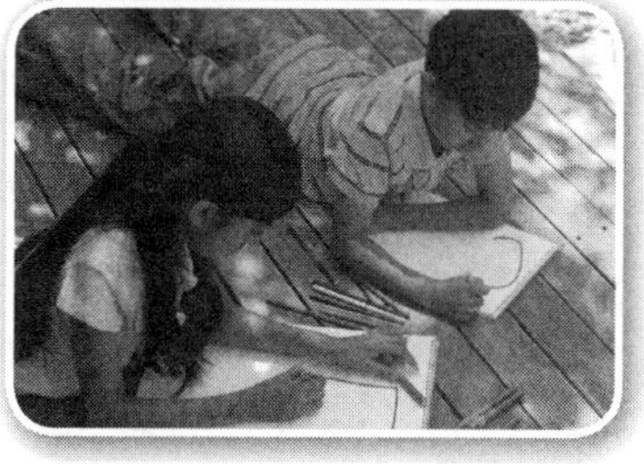

6. 

7. 

8. 

9. 

10. 

(10) sing ( ) stand up ( ) walk ( ) say ( ) listen

( ) write ( ) point ( ) read ( ) draw ( ) sit down

Unit 1

My Classroom

VOCABULARY I

1 **Listen and check.** Then ask and answer. Point. Work with a partner. **TR: 1.1**

2 **Look and write.**

a clock	a map
a board	a crayon
a computer	a pen
a classroom	a table
paper	a pencil

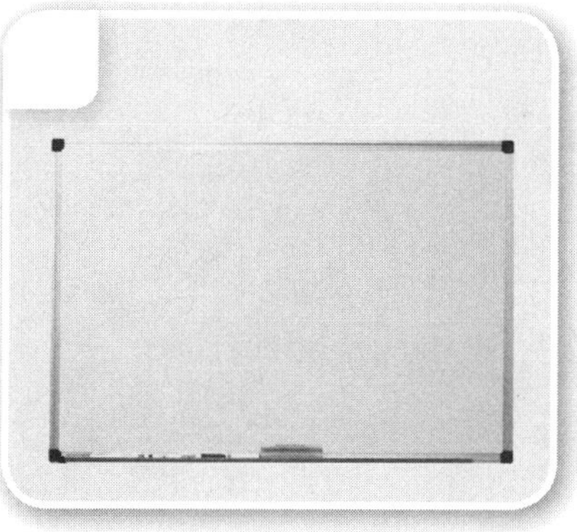

1. ____________________

2. ____________________

3. ____________________

4. ____________________

5. ____________________

6. ____________________

7. ____________________

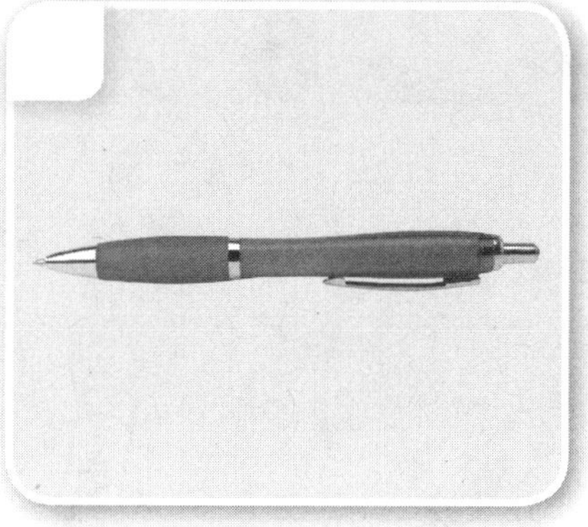

8. ____________________

9. ____________________

10. ____________________

SONG

1 **Listen to the song.** Circle. **TR: 1.2**

I have my   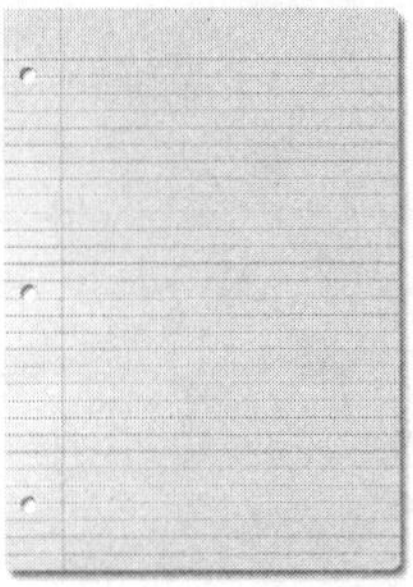 ,

and I have my 

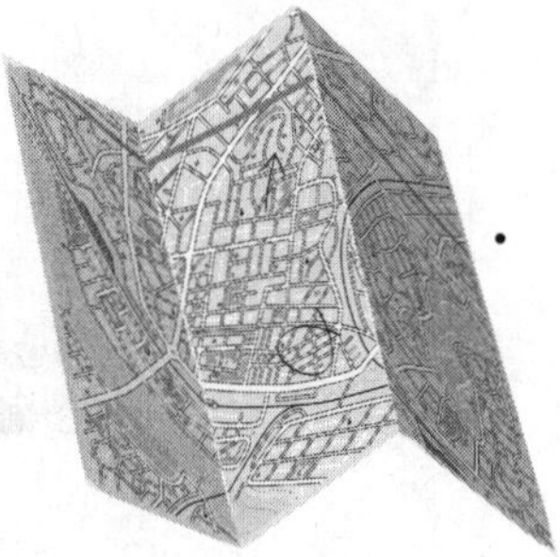 .

2 **Listen.** Write. **TR: 1.3**

We can count from one to ten.

1 2 ___ 4 ___ 6 7 ___ 9 ___

3 **Listen.** Color. **TR: 1.4**

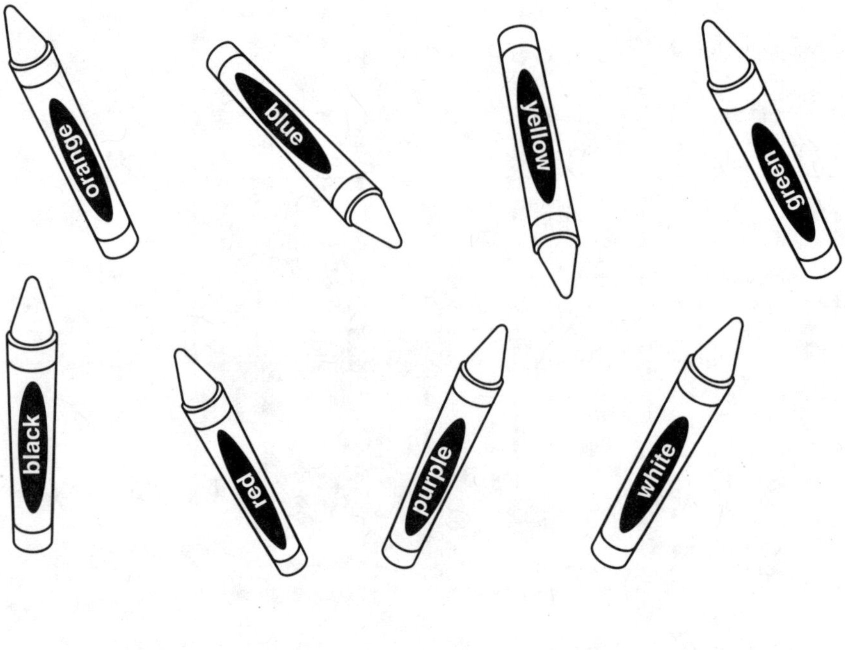

GRAMMAR I

Yes/No questions with *it's*

Question				Answer		
Is	it	an	eraser?	Yes, **it is.**	**It's** an eraser.	*It's = It is*
		a	pen?	No, **it isn't.**	**It's** a crayon.	*isn't = is not*

1 **Listen. Circle.** TR: 1.5

1.  Yes, it is. No, it isn't.

2.  Yes, it is. No, it isn't.

3.  Yes, it is. No, it isn't.

4.  Yes, it is. No, it isn't.

5.  Yes, it is. No, it isn't.

2 **Circle one word in the box.** Draw and color it. Then work with a partner. Ask and answer.

crayon paper pen table

3 **Look and draw lines.** Write.

a clock　　a computer　　a crayon　　a map　　a pen

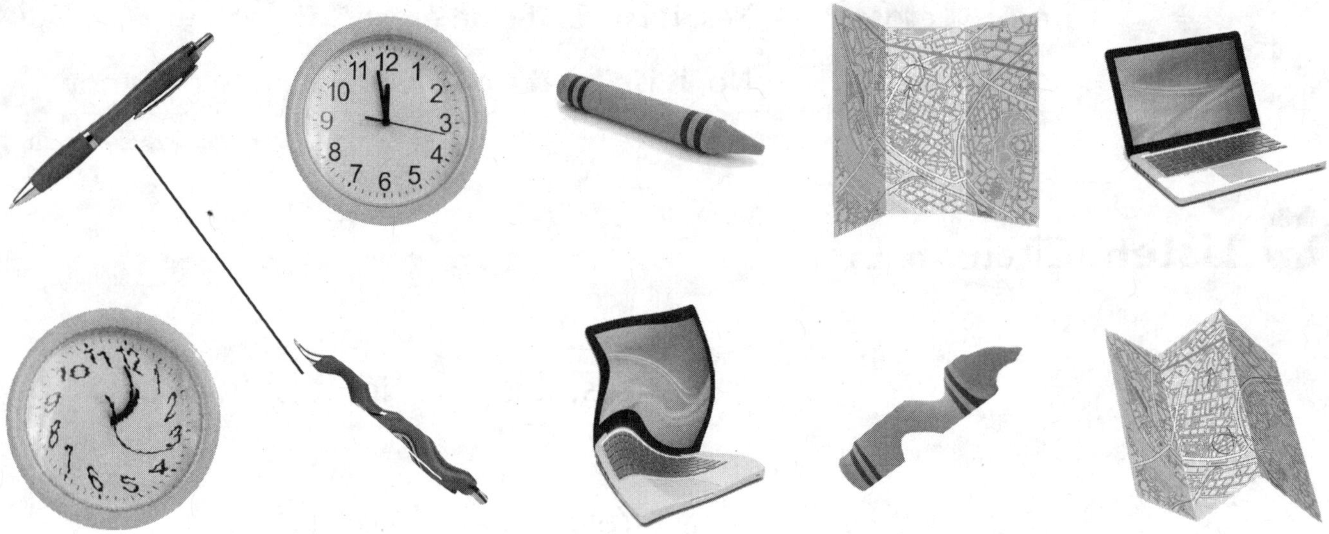

________　a pen　________　________　________

4 **Listen.** Look and read. Write. **TR: 1.6**

1. Is it a pencil?

   Yes, it is.

2. ________________?

   Yes, ________________.

3. ________________?

   No, ________________.

VOCABULARY 2

1 Read and match. Write the numbers.

(1)

( )

( )

( )

( )

1. an eraser 2. a book 3. a desk 4. a picture 5. a chair

2 Listen and find. Color. Write. **TR: 1.7**

1. picture
2. ______________________
3. ______________________
4. ______________________
5. ______________________

GRAMMAR 2

What* and *How many

Question				Answer
What		is	it?	It's an eraser.
	color	is	it?	It's orange.

Question	Answer
How many erasers?	Three.

1 **Listen and write.** Draw lines. TR: 1.8

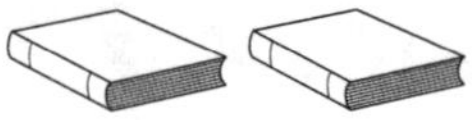

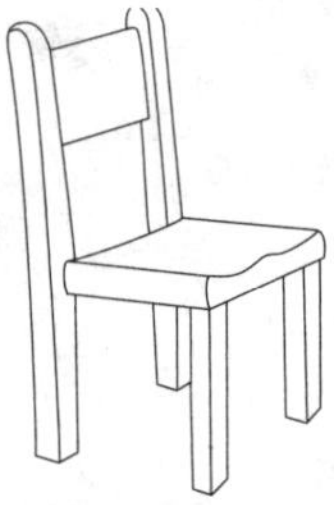

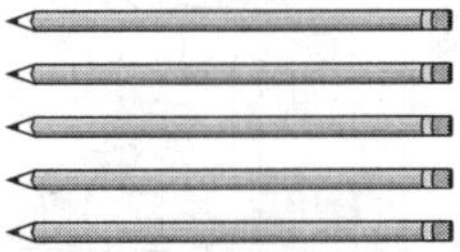

1. What is it?
2. __________ is the clock?
3. __________ pencils?
4. __________ is it?
5. __________ books?

2 **Look and write.**

1. In Vocabulary 2, Activity 2, it's gray. What is it? a picture
2. In Vocabulary 2, Activity 2, it's orange. What is it? __________
3. Look at Song, Activity 3. How many crayons? __________
4. In Vocabulary 2, Activity 2, it's green. What is it? __________

GAME TIME!

1 Listen and draw a line. TR: 1.9

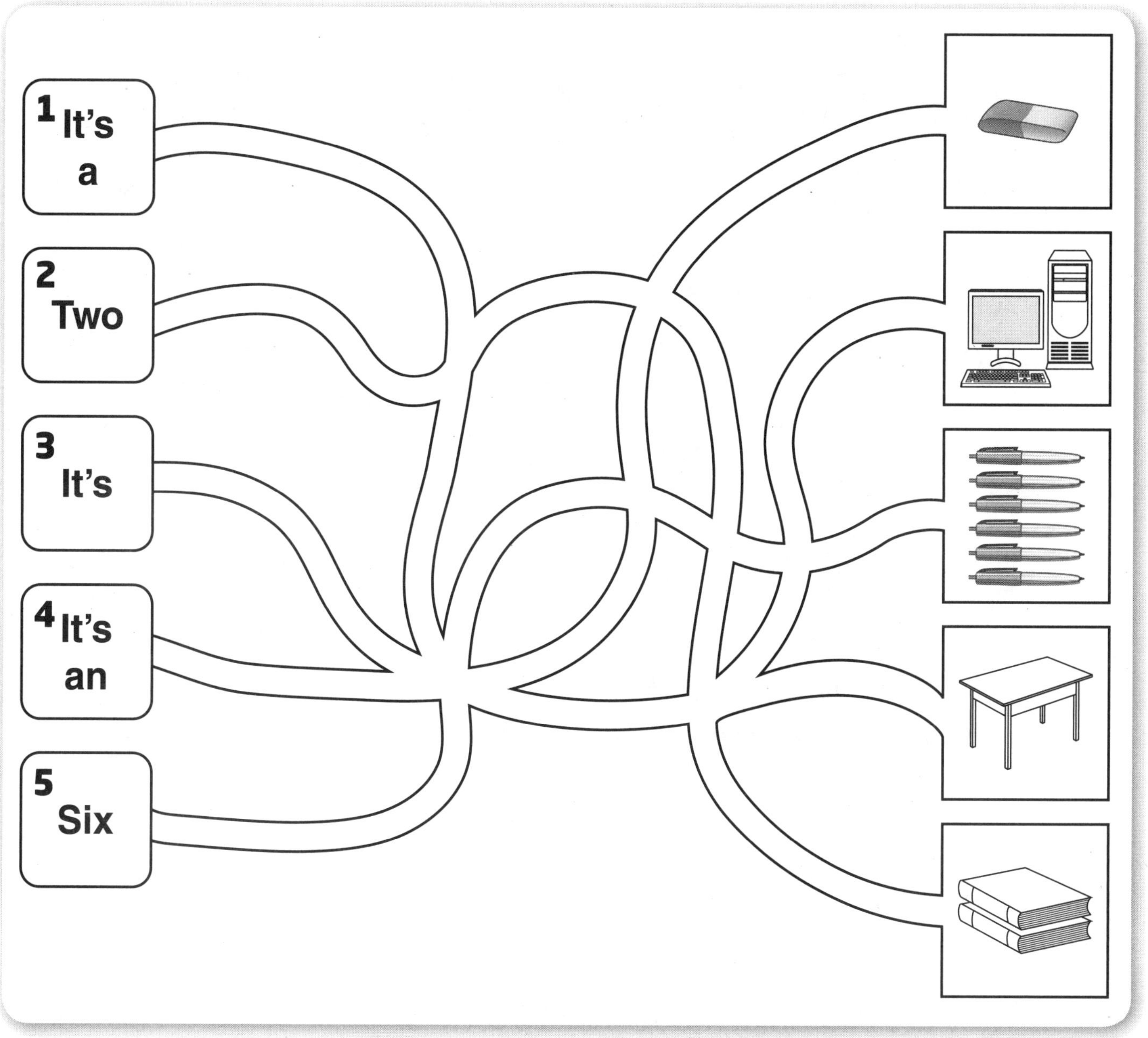

2 Cut out the letters in the back of the book.
Make words. Work with a partner.

How many words? ____________________

READING

1 Listen and read. TR: 1.10

The English Alphabet

In the past

A B C D E F G H I K L M
N O P Q R S T V X Y Z

23 letters

Now

A B C D E F G H I **J** K L M
N O P Q R S T **U** V **W** X Y Z

26 letters

2 Read. Circle yes or no.

1. Now the English alphabet has 20 letters. yes no
2. Letters represent sounds. yes no

3 Read and write.

1. In the past: How many letters? ____________
2. Now: How many letters? ____________

4 Read and write.

The English Alphabet	
In the past	A B C
Now	A

5 Listen and find. Color. TR: 1.11

WRITING

1 Write.

I'm is name What's your

Hello. My ______ ______ Sonia.

______ ______ name?

Hi. ______ Mark.

2 Look and write.

?	Is it a pencil? What is it?	What color is it? What's your name?
•	No, it's a map. It's a computer.	It's yellow. I'm Freddy.

1. Is it a clock ____
2. What is it ____
3. It's an eraser ____
4. What's your name ____
5. It's blue ____
6. How many desks ____

UNIT 1 REVIEW

1 Listen and circle. Color. TR: 1.12

1.

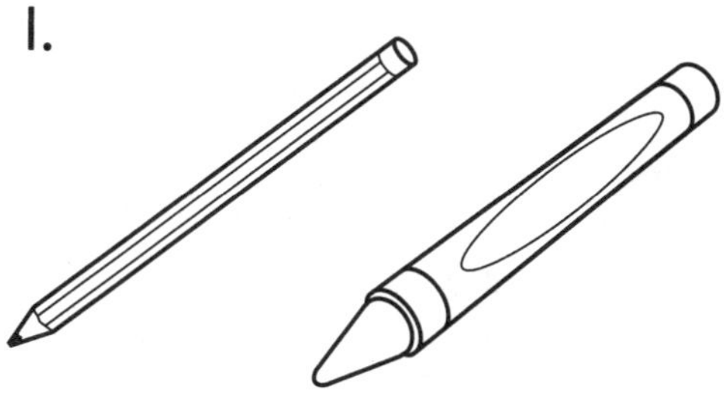

2.

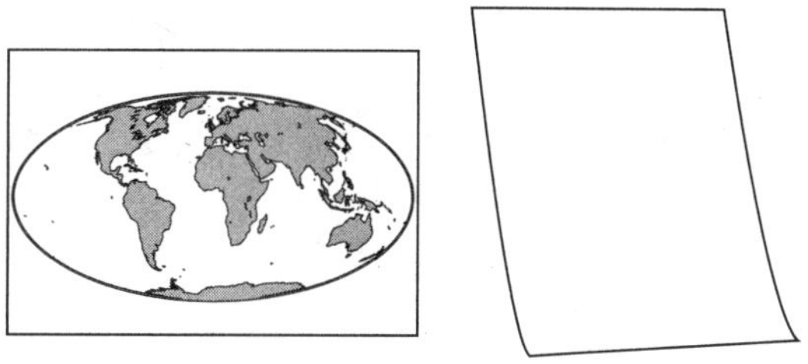

3.

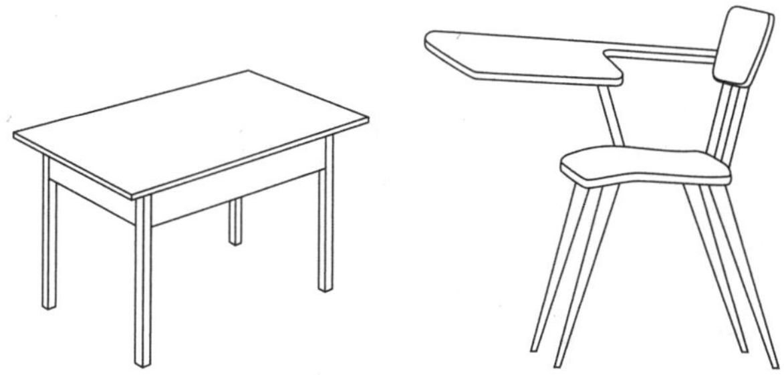

4.

5.

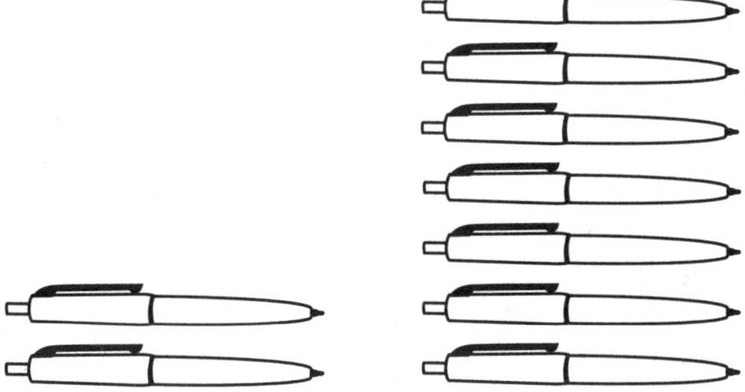

6.

Unit 2

My World

VOCABULARY I

1 **Listen and check.** Then ask and answer. Point. Work with a partner. **TR: 2.1**

2 **Look and write.**

a bird	a mountain	a rock	a tree
a butterfly	the ocean	the sky	
grass	a river	the sun	

1. ____________________

2. ____________________

3. ____________________

4. ____________________

5. ____________________

6. ____________________

7. ____________________

8. ____________________

9. ____________________

10. ____________________

SONG

1 Listen to the song. Circle. TR: 2.2

1. Where are the birds?
   Where are the sun and the moon?
   They're in the ______________.

2. Where are the fish?
   Where are the waves?
   They're in the ______________.

3. Where are the trees?
   Where are the rocks?
   They're in the ______________.

2 Listen. Write. TR: 2.3

mountains ocean sky

The rainbows and the ________________
and the ________________ and the ________________,
they are part of our world, part of our world.
Our beautiful world!

GRAMMAR I

to be: is, are

Question			Answer		
What	**is**	it?	**It's**	a tree.	*It's = It is*
	are	they?	**They're**	trees.	*They're = They are*

1 Write.

1. What ______are______ they?
2. What ______is______ it?
3. What ____________ they?
4. What ____________ it?
5. What ____________ it?
6. What ____________ they?

2 Write.

1. ______They're______ trees.
2. ______It's______ a river.
3. ____________ birds.
4. ____________ grass.
5. ____________ a mountain.
6. ____________ butterflies.

3 **Look and draw lines.** Write.

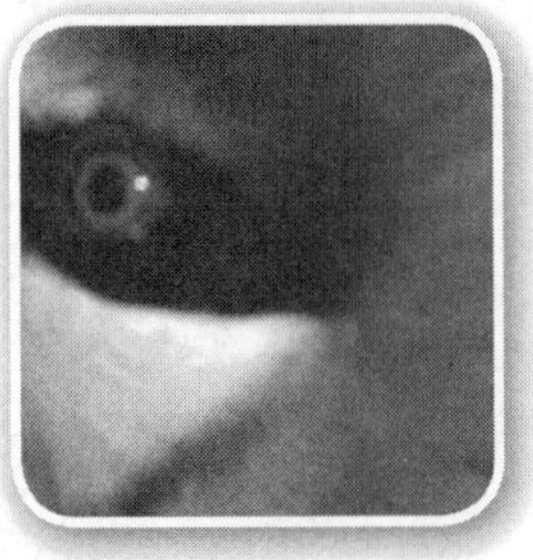

__________ butterflies __________ __________

4 **Listen and look.** Write. **TR: 2.4**

1. What are they?

   They're rocks.

2. __________?

   __________.

3. __________?

   __________.

VOCABULARY 2

1 **Read and match.** Write the numbers.

1. the moon 2. a star 3. a cloud 4. a bush 5. a flower

2 **Color.** Then work with a partner. Ask and answer.

What are they? They're ______________.

What is it? It's ______________.

GRAMMAR 2

Where* and *in* or *on

Question			Answer
Where	is	the moon?	It's **in** the sky.
	are	the birds?	They're **on** the rock.

1 Draw lines.

1. The butterfly is on the grass.
2. The clouds are in the sky.
3. The birds are in the tree.
4. The frog is in the river.
5. The flowers are on the bush.

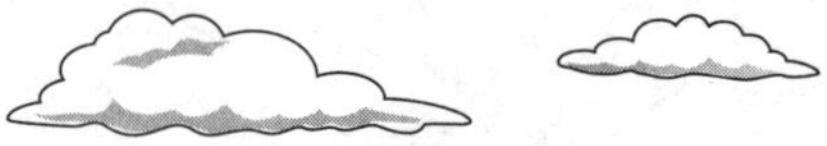

2 **Look at the pictures.** Write.

1. Where is ______ the butterfly?
2. Where are ______ the clouds?
3. ______ the birds?
4. ______ the frog?
5. ______ the flowers?

GAME TIME!

1 Look at the pictures. Circle the words.

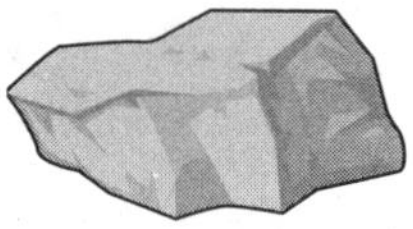

m	i	f	s	a	n	p	u	o	n	c
o	m	x	o	d	n	f	a	s	s	l
u	o	b	i	r	d	s	o	t	r	o
n	o	w	y	o	l	m	n	a	z	u
t	n	i	c	c	g	s	w	r	q	d
a	s	c	r	k	z	k	s	y	j	s
i	b	c	k	b	t	a	c	l	h	f
n	t	s	u	d	r	i	v	e	r	l
s	v	b	u	s	h	j	r	w	o	k
f	l	o	w	e	r	s	u	i	f	s

2 Look, read, and color. Then work with a partner. Ask and find.

bird
butterfly
flower
star

READING

1 Listen and read. TR: 2.5

The Northern Lights

Like rainbows, the Northern Lights show colors in the sky.

You see their colors at night.

2 Read. Circle **yes** or **no**.

1. You see the Northern Lights in the day. yes no
2. The Northern Lights are black and white. yes no

3 Read and circle.

1. A rainbow is in the sky. The ________________ is in the sky.

   a. moon b. sun

2. The Northern Lights are in the sky. The ____________ is in the sky.

   a. moon b. sun

4 Read and check.

	The Northern Lights	Rainbows
in the sky		
many colors		
in the day		
at night		

5 Color the picture.

WRITING

1 **Write.** Look at your picture on the previous page. Describe it.

1. The trees are ______________________.
2. The mountains are ______________________.
3. The stars are ______________________.
4. The sky is ______________________.
5. The Northern Lights are ______________________.

2 **Look and write.**

Big letter: **W I H F**	**W**hat is it? **W**hat color is it? **H**ow many trees?	**I**t's a tree. **I**t's green. **F**our trees.
Small letter: **w i h f**	W**hat is it**? W**hat color is it**? H**ow many trees**?	I**t's a tree**. I**t's green**. F**our trees**.

W w   H h   I i   T t   M m

1. ___hat's your name?
2. ___ow many pencils?
3. ___s it a butterfly?
4. ___he bird is in the tree.
5. ___ountains are big.

UNIT 2 REVIEW

1 Listen and circle. Color. TR: 2.6

1.

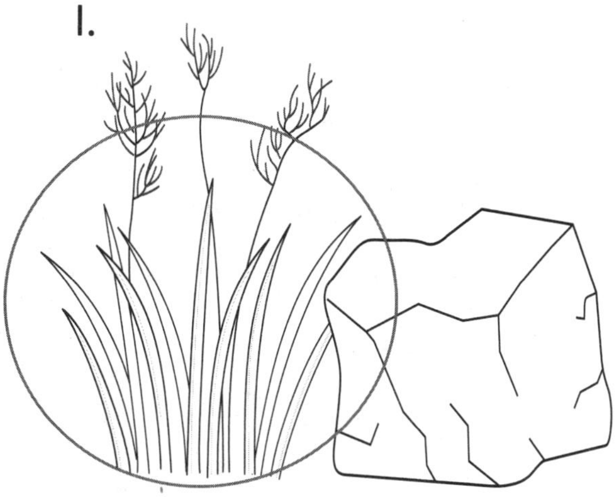

2.

3.

4.

5.

6.

Unit 3

My Family

VOCABULARY I

1 **Listen and check.** Then ask and answer. Point. Work with a partner. **TR: 3.1**

2 **Look and write.**

baby	grandfather	a photo
brother	grandmother	sister
family	mother	
father	parents	

1. ______________________
2. ______________________
3. ______________________
4. ______________________
5. ______________________
6. ______________________
7. ______________________
8. ______________________
9. ______________________
10. ______________________

9
10
6
4
2
5
1
7
8
3

SONG

1 **Listen to the song.** Check. **TR: 3.2**

	Family in the song	Your family
big	✓	
small		
big brother		
big sister		
little brother		
little sister		
baby brother		
baby sister		
2 boys		
2 girls		

2 **Listen.** Write. **TR: 3.3**

all
big
short
tall

Some are ______________,

and some are ______________.

I have a ______________ family,

and I love them ______________!

GRAMMAR I

to have

Question	Answer			
How many sisters do you have?	I	**have**	one sister.	
		don't have	any sisters.	*don't = do not*

1 Listen. Circle. TR: 3.4

1. I have two brothers. — I have two sisters.
2. I don't have any sisters. — I don't have any brothers.
3. One. I have a baby brother. — One. I have a baby sister.
4. I don't have a big sister. — I don't have a big brother.

2 Look and listen. Write. TR: 3.5

baby   big   brother   family   sister

Hi, I'm Lisa. I have a big ______________.

I have a ______________ brother.

I have a little ______________.

I have a big ______________.

And I have a ______________ sister, too!

3 **Look at Miguel's family.** Read and write.

Juana—mother

Ana—grandmother

Angel—father

Paco—grandfather

Pablo—brother

Rosa—sister

Luis—brother

Lola—baby sister

1. Is Miguel's family big or small? ____________
2. How many brothers? ____________
3. How many sisters? ____________

4 **What about your family?** Draw and write.

1. How many sisters do you have?

   I ____________________.

2. How many brothers do you have?

   I ____________________.

VOCABULARY 2

1 **Look and read.** Circle.

1. tall short

2. tall short

3. young old

4. young old

5. small big

6. small big

2 **Read.** Draw and color.

a big book

an old grandmother

a tall tree

a small book

a young boy

a short tree

GRAMMAR 2

He/She and questions with *who*

Question		Answer	*Who's = Who is*
Who's	he?	**He's** my brother Jack.	*He's = He is*
	she?	**She's** my sister Ana.	*She's = She is*

1 **Listen.** Write the number. **TR: 3.6**

1

2 **Look at the photos.** Write.

1. She's my sister.
2. He's my ____________.
3. She's my ____________.
4. She's my ____________, and he's my baby ____________.
5. He's my ____________.
6. He's my ____________.

GAME TIME!

1 **Listen.** Draw a line. TR: 3.7

2 **What is the secret message?** Look at the letters and numbers. Write the letters.

A	B	C	D	E	F	
1	2	3	4	5	6	
G	H	I	J	K	L	
7	8	9	10	11	12	
M	N	O	P	Q	R	S
13	14	15	16	17	18	19
T	U	V	W	X	Y	Z
20	21	22	23	24	25	26

9   12 15 22 5   13 25   6 1 13 9 12 25

__   __ __ __ __   __ __   __ __ __ __ __ __.

READING

1 Listen and read. TR: 3.8

Families Around the World

Families are different. They are big or small. Families live in different places, too.

a family in China

a family in Australia

This small family lives in China. And this small family lives in Australia. This big family lives in Ethiopia.

a family in Ethiopia

2 Read. Circle **yes** or **no**.

1. The small families live in China and Ethiopia. yes no
2. The big family lives in Ethiopia. yes no
3. Families are different. yes no

3 Look at the chart. Read. Check.

Family	Big	Small
in China		✓
in Australia		
in Ethiopia		
your family		

4 Read. Look at the photos on the left. Write.

1. The family in China is ______________.
2. The family in Australia is ______________.
3. The family in Ethiopia is ______________.
4. The family in China has ______________ baby.
5. The family in China has ______________ parents.
6. The family in Australia has ______________ baby.
7. The family in Ethiopia has ______________ babies.

WRITING

1 Look at the picture.
Pretend you are the person in the middle. Write about "your" family.

1. Hi. My name is ____________________.

2. In this picture, you see my ____________________.

3. I have a ______________ family.

4. My father is ______________, and my mother is ______________.

5. I have two brothers and two ______________.

2 Look and write.

Who?	**I**	have one brother.
	My father	is tall.
	You	have five crayons.
What?	**The flower**	is yellow.
	The tree	is tall.
	The map	is on the table.

1. __________ have three sisters.
2. ______________ is short.
3. ______________ is green.
4. ______________ is on the desk.

UNIT 3 REVIEW

1 Listen and circle. TR: 3.9

1.

brother sister

2.

grandfather grandmother

3.

father mother

4.

old young

5.

small big

6.

tall short

Review: Units 1–3

1 **Look.** Listen and circle. **TR: R1.1**

1.  

2.  

3.  

4.  

5.  

2 Look and write.

1. What color is the rock? It's ________________.
2. What color are the clouds? They're ________________.
3. How many flowers? ________________ flowers.
4. Where is the sun? It's ________________.
5. Where are the birds? They're ________________.

3 Listen and read. Circle. TR: R1.2

1. How many brothers do you have?	How many sisters do you have?
2. I don't have any sisters.	I have four sisters.
3. Who's he?	Who's she?
4. She's my baby sister.	He's my baby brother.
5. He's young.	He's old.
6. I have a small family.	I have a big family.

Unit 4

My House

VOCABULARY I

1 **Listen and check.** Then ask and answer. Point. Work with a partner. **TR: 4.1**

1. ______________________

2. ______________________

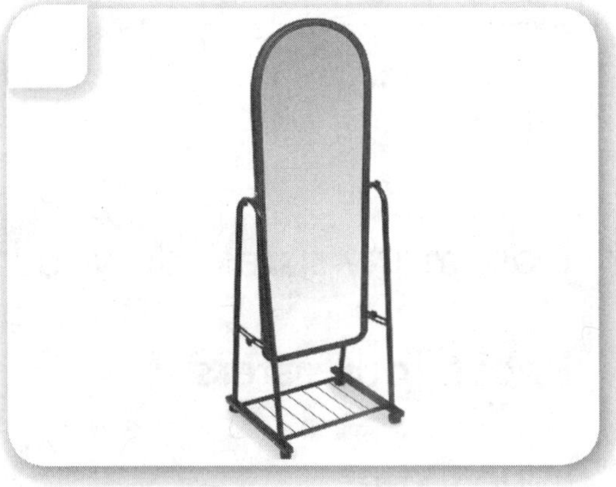

3. ______________________

4. ______________________

5. ______________________

6. ______________________

7. ______________________

8. ______________________

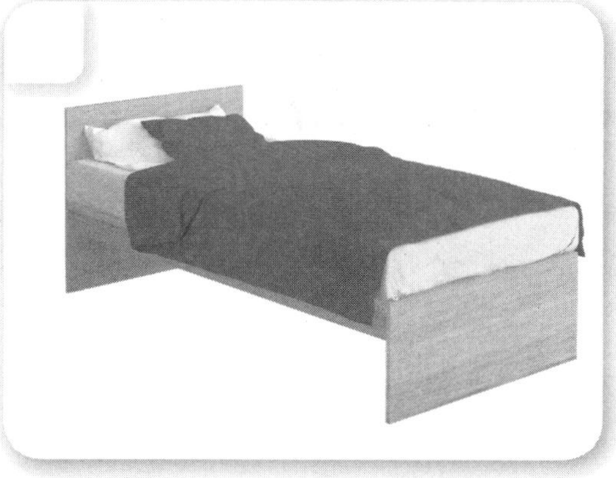

9. ______________________

10. ______________________

2 Look and write.

a bathroom	a dining room	a living room	a TV
a bed	a kitchen	a mirror	
a bedroom	a lamp	a sofa	

SONG

1 **Listen to the song.** Circle. **TR: 4.2**

1. Where do you sleep?

   I sleep in the ______.

   Is there a ______?

   Yes, there is.

2. Where do you eat?

   I eat in the ______.

   Is there a spoon?

   Yes, there is.

2 **Write a new verse for the song.** Use words from the boxes.

read sit down	bedroom dining room kitchen living room	bed chair sofa

Where do you ______________?

I ______________ in the ______________.

Is there a ______________?

Yes, there is.

GRAMMAR I

Yes / No* questions with *Is there . . . ?

Question			Answer	
Is there	a lamp	in the bedroom?	Yes, **there is.**	*isn't = is not*
	a TV	in the kitchen?	No, **there isn't.**	

1 Listen. Circle. TR: 4.3

1. Yes, there is.   No, there isn't.
2. Yes, there is.   No, there isn't.
3. Yes, there is.   No, there isn't.
4. Yes, there is.   No, there isn't.
5. Yes, there is.   No, there isn't.
6. Yes, there is.   No, there isn't.
7. Yes, there is.   No, there isn't.
8. Yes, there is.   No, there isn't.

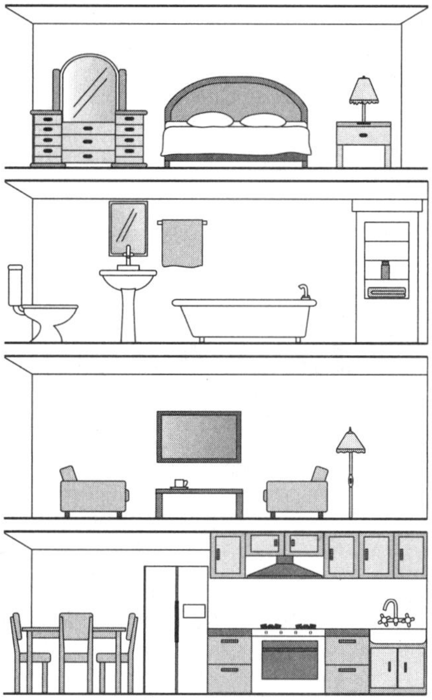

2 Look and listen. Write. TR: 4.4

1. Is there a TV in the living room?

   Yes, there is.

2. ______________ a bed in the kitchen?

   ____

3. ______________ a lamp in the bathroom?

   ____

4. ______________ a lamp in the living room?

   ____

3 Circle one room in the list. Draw it.

bedroom
dining room
kitchen
living room

4 Write about your picture.

1. What is your picture?

   It's a ______________________________.

2. Is there a table in your picture?

   ____

3. Is there a sofa in your picture?

   ____

4. Is there a mirror in your picture?

   ____

5. Is there a lamp in your picture?

   ____

VOCABULARY 2

1 **Look.** Read. Match. Draw lines.

a. Who's cooking?

b. Who's watching TV?

c. Who's cleaning?

d. Who's sleeping?

e. Who's eating?

f. Who's taking a bath?

1.

2.
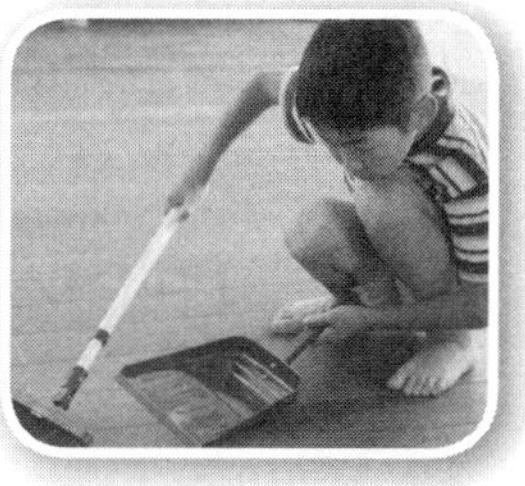

3.

4.

5.

6.

2 **Find and answer.** Then compare your answers with a partner.

1. She's watching TV. ________

2. He's cleaning. ________

GRAMMAR 2

Present progressive: *He / She is* + verb-*ing*

Question	Answer
Where is your sister?	She's in the kitchen.

Question			Answer		
What's	she	**doing?**	She's	**eating.**	*What's = What is* *She's = She is*

1 **Listen.** Circle. **TR: 4.5**

1. She's cleaning. She's cooking.
2. He's sleeping. He's cleaning.
3. She's watching TV. She's taking a bath.
4. He's taking a bath. He's eating.

2 **Look at the photos.** Write.

1. Where's the baby?

   She's in the bedroom. She's sleeping.

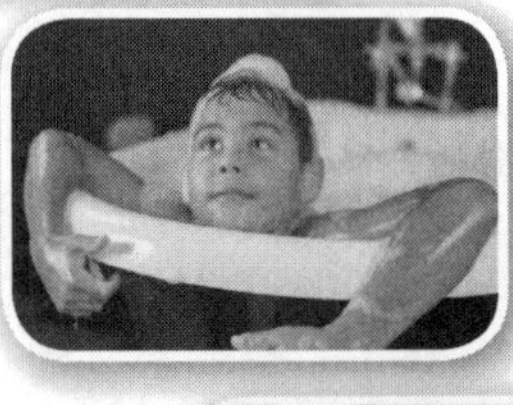

2. ________ the brother?

   He's in the bathroom. He's ________.

3. ________ the grandmother?

   She's in the kitchen. She's ________.

4. ________ the father?

   He's in the living room. He's ________.

GAME TIME!

1 **Color.** Then work with a partner. Ask and find.

boy	girl	lamp
mirror	sofa	TV

2 **Look at the picture.** Read. Write.

1. Where's the girl?

   She's in the ______________. She's ______________.

2. Where's the boy?

   He's in the ______________. He's ______________.

READING

1 Listen and read. TR: 4.6

A House in the Trees

This house is in the trees. It is a tree house! A tree house can have a living room, a kitchen, and a bedroom.

a tree house

Is there a bedroom in the tree house?

2 Read. Circle yes or no.

1. A tree house is in the sky. yes no
2. There is a bedroom in the tree house. yes no

3 **Look and read.** Write.

Where is it?

____

tree house

What rooms can it have?

a living room

____

____

4 **Read and write.**

1. Where is a tree house?

____

2. What can a tree house have?

____

____

5 **Draw a tree house.** Write.

What rooms does your tree house have?

____

____

____

____

WRITING

1 **Look at the picture.** You are on the sofa. Color the sofa green. Color the lamp yellow. Color the TV black. Write about your living room.

1. Hi, I'm ______________.
2. In this picture, I am on the green ______________.
3. I am in the ______________.
4. There is a yellow ______________.
5. There is a black __________.
6. I am ______________ TV.

2 **Look and write.**

Big letter: **W** **I**	**W**here's your father**?** **I**s he in the kitchen**?**	**?**
Big letter: **Y** **T** **H**	**Y**es, he's in the kitchen. **T**his is my father. **H**e's cooking.	**.**

1. ___here's your sister___
2. ___s she in the dining room___
3. ___es, she's in the dining room___
4. ___he's eating___

UNIT 4 REVIEW

1 **Look.** Read and circle.

1. Is there a man in the kitchen?

   Yes, there is. No, there isn't.

2. Is there a lamp in the dining room?

   Yes, there is. No, there isn't.

3. Where's the sofa?

   It's in the dining room. It's in the living room.

4. Where's the girl?

   She's in the dining room. She's in the living room.

2 **Circle and draw.**

There is a **frog / monkey** in the **bedroom / living room**.

It's **cleaning / sleeping**.

Unit 5

Cool Clothes

VOCABULARY I

1 **Listen and check.** Then ask and answer. Point. Work with a partner. **TR: 5.1**

2 **Look and write.**

a dress	a shirt
gloves	shoes
a hat	a skirt
a jacket	socks
pants	a T-shirt

1. ____________________

2. ____________________

3. ____________________

4. ____________________

5. ____________________

6. ____________________

7. ____________________

8. ____________________

9. ____________________

10. ____________________

SONG

1 **Listen to the song.** Read and write. Draw lines to match. Color. **TR: 5.2**

1. I'm wearing my brown

   ________________,

   and I really like them.

2. I'm wearing my purple

   ________________,

   and I really like them.

3. I'm wearing my orange

   ________________,

   and I really like it.

4. I'm wearing my pink

   ________________,

   and I really like it.

2 **Write a new verse for the song!**
Use words from the box.

dress	gloves	hat	jacket
shoes	skirt	socks	T-shirt

I like my ________________! I like my ________________!

I like my ________________! I like my ________________!

GRAMMAR I

Present progressive: *am / are / is* + verb-*ing*

<table>
<tr><th colspan="4">Question</th><th colspan="4">Answer</th></tr>
<tr><td rowspan="2">What</td><td>are</td><td>you</td><td rowspan="2">wearing?</td><td>I'm</td><td rowspan="2">wearing</td><td>white shoes.</td><td rowspan="2">I'm = I am
He's = He is
She's = She is</td></tr>
<tr><td>is</td><td>your brother
the girl</td><td>He's
She's</td><td>a hat.</td></tr>
</table>

1 **Listen.** Read and write. **TR: 5.3**

1. What __________ you wearing?

   I'm wearing a skirt.

2. What are you wearing?

   __________ __________ a jacket.

3. What are you __________?

   I'm wearing a T-shirt.

4. What is your brother wearing?

   My __________ wearing pants.

2 **Listen.** Look at the chart. Read. Check. **TR: 5.4**

	Mother	Father
skirt		
dress		
pants		
socks		
shoes		
shirt		

3 **Draw your partner.** Then ask and answer with a partner.

4 Write about your picture.

1. What is ______________________________ wearing?
2. ________ wearing ______________________________

____

____.

VOCABULARY 2

1 **Look at the picture.** Write. Use words from the box.

closet
gloves
shelf
skirt

____

____

____

____

2 **Listen.** Look at the picture. Color. **TR: 5.5**

3 **Look at the picture.** Read and write.

1. Where is the shelf?

____

2. Where are the gloves?

____

3. What color is the hat?

____

4. What color are the shoes?

____

5. What color is the skirt?

____

GRAMMAR 2

Questions with *that* and *those*

Question		Answer		
What's	**that?**	**That's**	my pink hat.	*What's = What is*
What are	**those?**	**Those are**	my brown pants.	*That's = That is*

1 **Listen.** Write the number. **TR: 5.6**

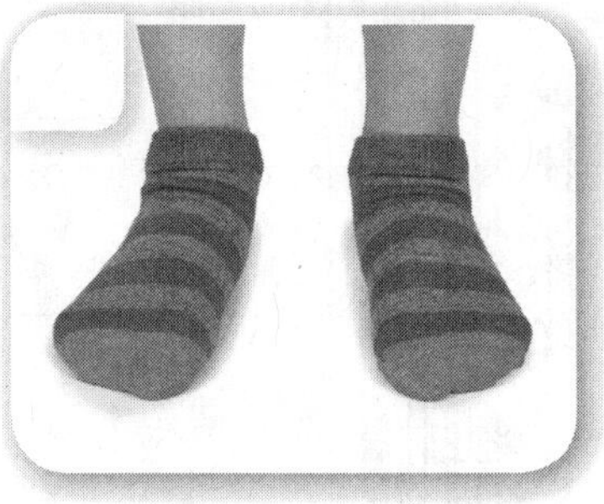

2 **Listen again.** Read and write. **TR: 5.7**

1. What's that ?
   That's my dress.
2. What ______________?
   Those are my socks.
3. What are those?
   ______________ my gloves.
4. ______________ that?
   ______________ my jacket.
5. What's ______________?
   That's my shirt.
6. What ______________?
   Those are my shoes.

GAME TIME!

1 **Play a game.** Cut out the cards and the closet on page 121. Color the cards. Put them in the closet and on the shelf. Play with a partner. Point. Ask and answer.

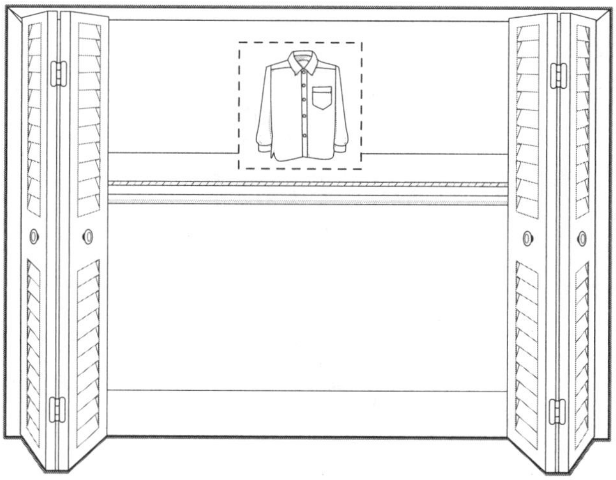

2 **Listen and draw a line.** TR: 5.8

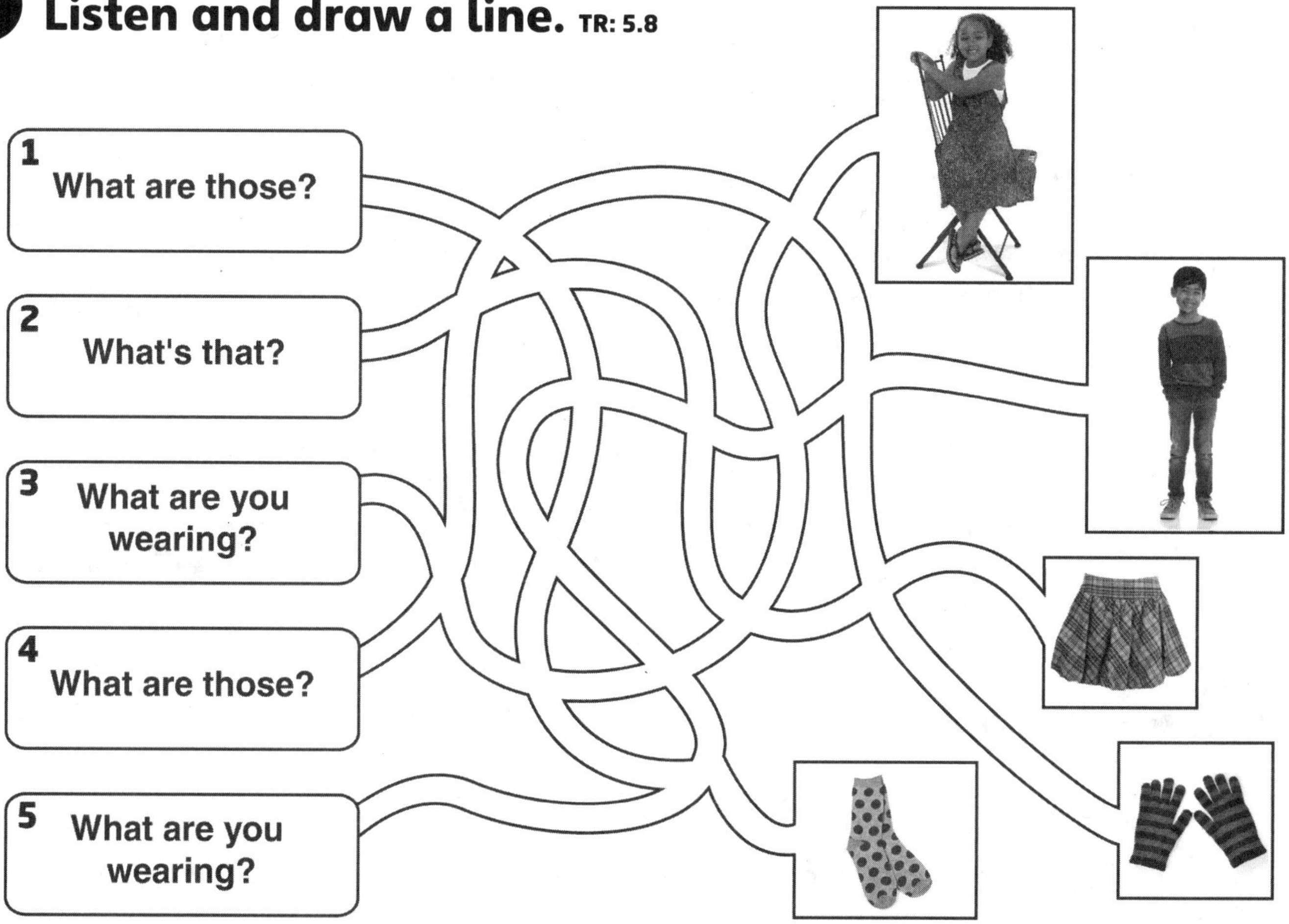

READING

1 **Listen and read.** TR: 5.9

Clothes for Work

People all over the world wear special clothes to work. Some people wear gloves and hats to work.

A chef wears special clothes for cooking.

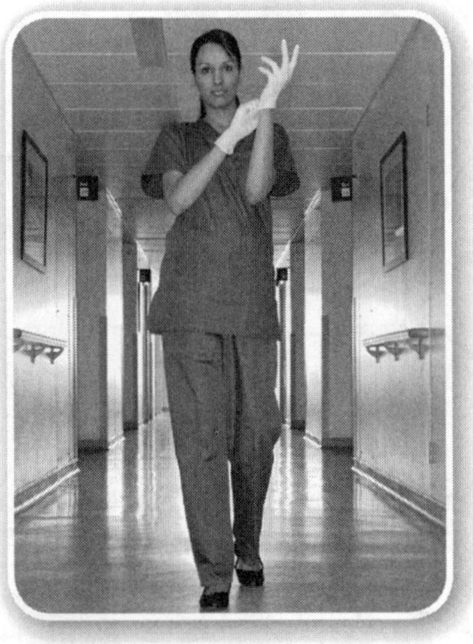

a doctor

a builder

a police officer

2 **Read.** Look. Circle **yes** or **no.**

1. The chef wears a tall hat to cook. yes no
2. The chef wears gloves. yes no

3 **Look at Activity 1.** Read. Check ✓ the clothes.

	chef	doctor	builder	police officer
hat				
gloves				
shirt				
T-shirt				
pants				
shoes				
skirt				
jacket				

4 Read and write.

1. The chef is wearing ____

____.

2. The doctor is wearing ____

____.

3. The builder is wearing ____

____.

4. The police officer is wearing ____

____.

5 **Write.** What do you wear to school? Then ask a partner and write.

I wear ____ to school.

______________________ wears ____.

WRITING

1 Look at the picture.
Write about the clothes.

1. The chef is wearing a tall white ________.

2. She is wearing a white ________.

3. She is wearing black and white ________.

4. She is wearing two black ________.

2 Write about the clothes in your closet.
Use color words.

black	blue	brown	green	pink
purple	red	white	yellow	

____

____

____

____

____

UNIT 5 REVIEW

1 **Color.** Read and write.

1. What's that?

____

2. What are those?

____

3. What is the boy wearing?

____

4. What is the girl wearing?

____

5. What color is the skirt?

____

6. What is in the closet?

____

Unit 6

My Toys

VOCABULARY I

1 **Listen and check.** Then ask and answer. Point. Work with a partner. TR: 6.1

2 **Look and write.**

a ball	a kite
a bike	a puppet
a car	a top
a drum	a train
a game	a truck

1. ____________________

2. ____________________

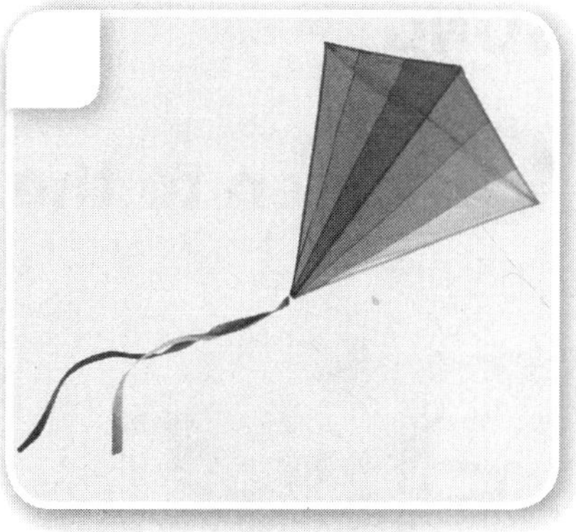

3. ____________________

4. ____________________

5. ____________________

6. ____________________

7. ____________________

8. ____________________

9. ____________________

10. ____________________

SONG

1 **Listen to the song.** Check. TR: 6.2

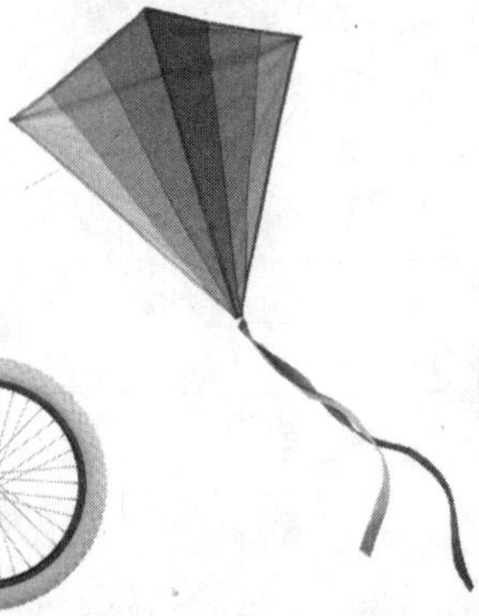

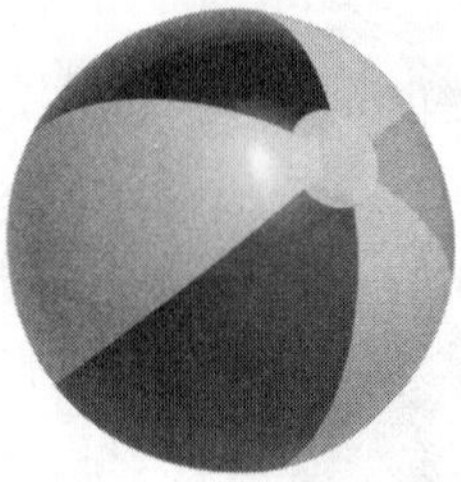

Do you want to . . . ?	Yes, I do.	No, I don't.
bang on a drum		
ride a bike		
fly a kite		
dress my doll		
kick a ball		
play with trains		

2 **Listen.** Write. TR: 6.3

ball   bike   doll   drum   kite   trains

1. Do you want to bang on a ____________?
2. Do you want to ride a ____________?
3. Do you want to fly a ____________?
4. Do you want to dress my ____________?
5. Do you want to kick a ____________?
6. Do you want to play with ____________?

GRAMMAR I

Simple present of *want*: *I / you / he, she*

Question				Answer	
Do	you	**want**	a bike?	Yes, I **do**.	*don't = do not*
				No, I **don't**. I **want** a train.	
Does	he/she			Yes, she **does**.	*doesn't = does not*
				No, he **doesn't**. She **wants** a train.	

1 Listen and read. Circle. TR: 6.4

1. Yes, I do. No, I don't.
2. Yes, I do. No, I don't.
3. Yes, she does. No, she doesn't.
4. Yes, he does. No, he doesn't.
5. Yes, I do. No, I don't.
6. Yes, she does. No, she doesn't.

2 Listen and read.
Draw a line. TR: 6.5

1. Do you want a car?
2. Does she want a drum?
3. Does he want a ball?
4. Do you want a train?

No, I don't.
I want a bike.

Yes, I do.
I want a car.

Yes, she does.
She wants a drum.

No, he doesn't.
He wants a kite.

3 **Listen.** Write. TR: 6.6

1. Do you want a ball?

   No, I don't.

2. ______ she want a truck?

   No, she ______.

3. ______ she want a train?

   Yes, she ______.

4. ______ you want a bike?

   Yes, I ______.

4 **Look.** Read and write.

1. Does the boy want a truck? No, he doesn't.
2. Does the girl want a bike? ______
3. Does the boy want a ball? ______
4. Does the boy want a drum? ______
5. Does the girl want a train? ______

VOCABULARY 2

1 **Look at the picture.** Write.

board game   doll   puzzle   robot   teddy bear

2 **What about you?** Read. Check ✓. Then ask a partner.

	I want	I don't want	My partner wants	My partner doesn't want
a doll				
a teddy bear				
a board game				
a robot				
a puzzle				

GRAMMAR 2

Questions with *this* and *these*

Question		Answer	
Is **this**	your puzzle?	Yes, **it** is.	*isn't = is not*
		No, **it** isn't. **It's** Marco's puzzle.	*It's = It is*
Are **these**	your dolls?	Yes, **they** are.	*aren't = are not*
		No, **they** aren't. **They're** Anita's dolls.	*They're = They are*

1 Read and write.

1. ________________ your robot?
2. ________________ your teddy bears?
3. ________________ your puzzles?
4. ________________ your board game?
5. ________________ your robots?
6. ________________ Mia's puppet?
7. ________________ Anya's drum?
8. ________________ Ivan's puzzles?

2 Listen and write. TR: 6.7

1. Yes, __________ is.
2. No, __________ aren't.
3. No, __________ aren't.
4. No, __________ isn't.
5. Yes, __________ are.
6. No, __________ isn't.
7. Yes, __________ is.
8. Yes, __________ are.

GAME TIME!

1 **Play a game.** Cut out the game boards and cards on page 123. Take a card. Read the word. Match the word to the picture. Play with a partner. Take turns.

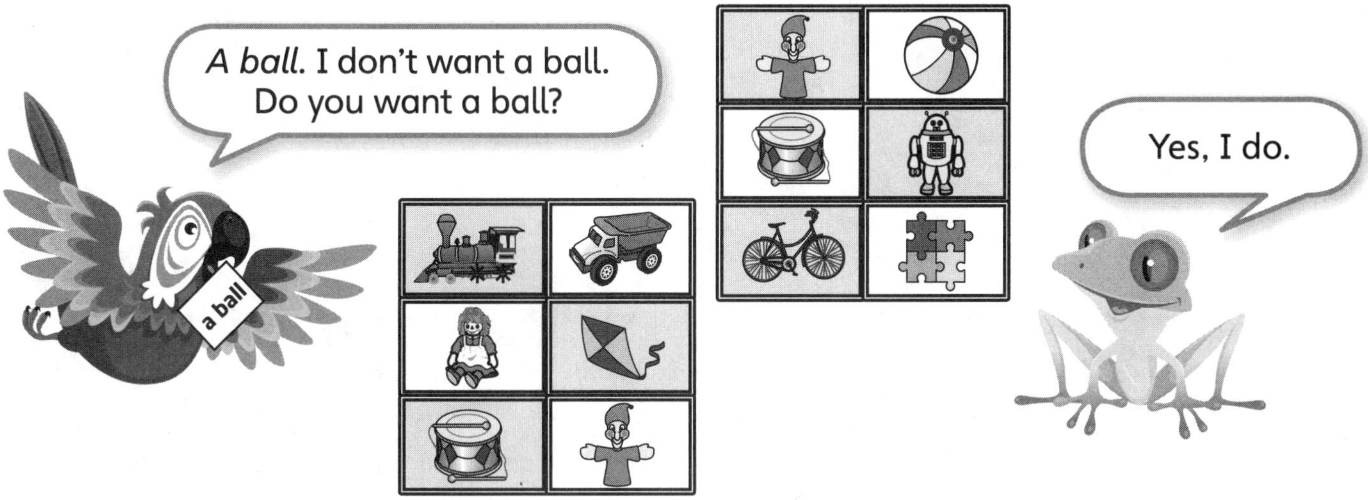

2 **Look at the photos.** Circle the words.

g	a	m	e	t	b	i	c	k	l
a	z	o	m	u	i	z	c	a	r
n	t	r	u	c	k	a	z	k	o
e	r	d	o	b	e	l	o	i	b
b	a	l	l	x	l	a	f	t	o
k	i	s	r	p	u	p	p	e	t
s	n	f	p	u	z	z	l	e	e
u	g	d	r	u	m	m	a	s	l
m	d	o	l	l	u	z	z	m	p

READING

1 Listen and read. TR: 6.8

We ❤ Kites

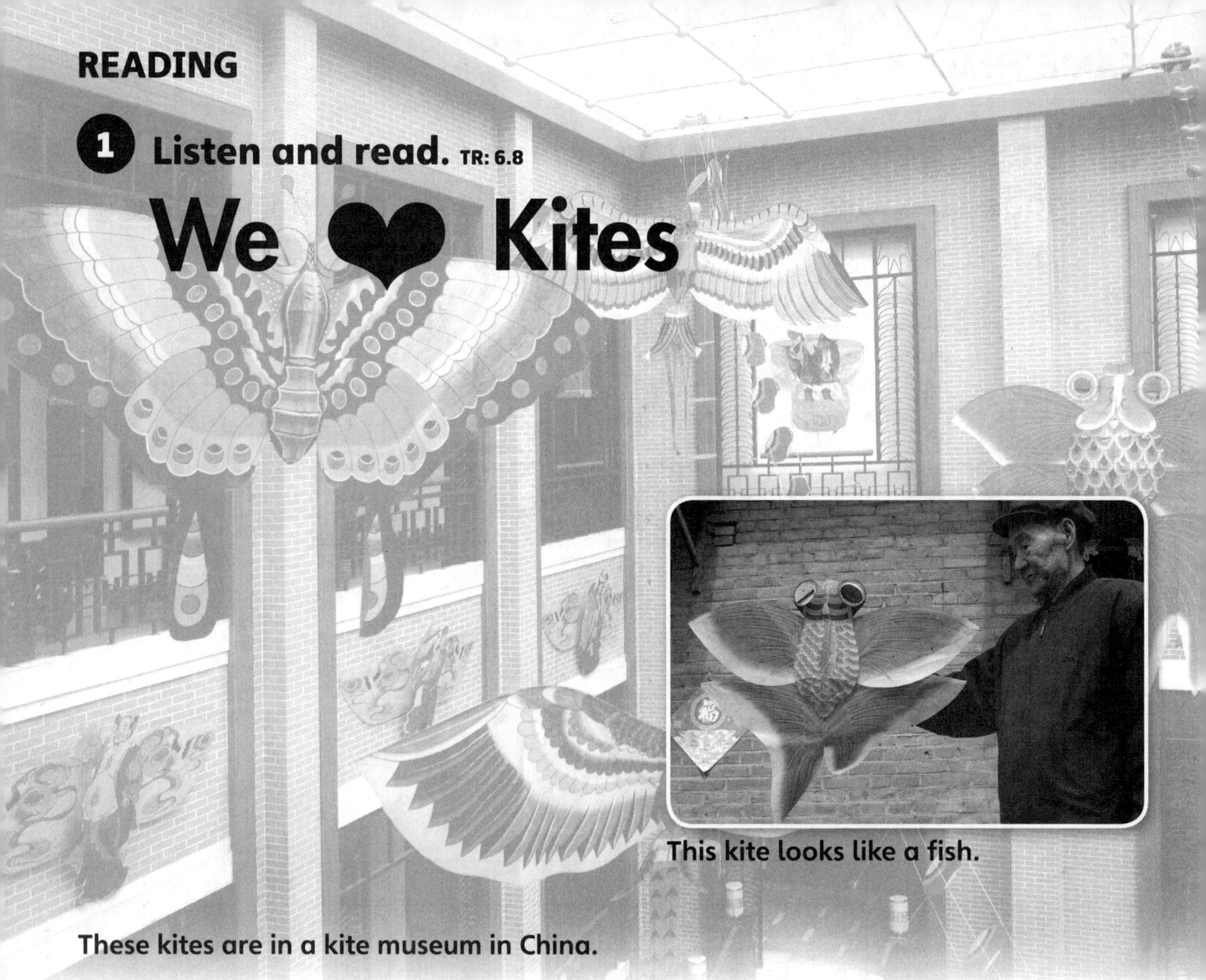

This kite looks like a fish.

These kites are in a kite museum in China.

People around the world love kites. People fly kites. There are even kite museums! This kite museum is in China. It has big kites and small kites. Some kites look like birds. Some kites look like butterflies. Some kites look like fish!

2 Read. Look. Circle yes or no.

1. There are kite museums. yes no
2. This museum is in China. yes no
3. There are robots and trains in the museum. yes no

3 **Look and read.** Write.

Kite Museum

Where

____

What

big kites

____

fish kites

____

____

4 **Look and read.** Match. Write the number.

1. This kite is a bird.
2. A butterfly is on this kite.
3. This kite is a teddy bear.

WRITING

1 **Look at the picture.** Write about the toys.

1. A ____________________, a ____________________, and a ____________________ are on the shelf.

2. A ____________________ and a ____________________ are on the table.

3. There is a big ____________________.

4. The girl wants a ____________________.

5. The boy wants a ____________________.

2 **What do you want?** Draw a toy you want. Write about it.

This is a toy I want.

What is it? It's a ____________________.

Is it big or small? It's ____________________.

What color is it? This ____________________ is ____________________.

UNIT 6 REVIEW

1 Listen and circle. TR: 6.9

Yes, he does.

No, he doesn't.

Yes, she does.

No, she doesn't.

Is this your robot?

Are these your robots?

No, it isn't.
It's Mateo's car.

No, they aren't.
They're Mateo's cars.

No, I don't.
I want a car.

Yes, I do.
I want a puppet.

Do you want a truck?
Do you want a train?

Review: Units 4–6

1 Listen and read. Circle. TR: R2.1

1. He's in the bathroom.	He's in the bedroom.
2. I'm wearing a pink shirt.	I'm wearing a pink skirt.
3. That's my brown truck.	Those are my brown tops.
4. Those are my dolls.	Those are my balls.
5. No, I don't.	Yes, I do.
6. No, he doesn't.	Yes, he does.

2 Listen and write. TR: R2.2

1. ____________ your hat?
   No, ____________ isn't.
   It's my mother's hat.

2. ____________ your pants?
   No, ____________ aren't.
   They're my brother's pants.

3. What's that?
   ____________ my robot.

4. What ____________?
   Those are my socks.

3 **Listen.** Look at the picture. Color. TR: R2.3

4 **Look at the picture.** Write.

1. The mother is in the ________. She's ________.

2. A ________ and ________ are on the sofa.

3. A jacket is in the ________.

4. Is there a teddy bear on the shelf?

   ________, there ________.

5. Is there a TV in the living room?

   ________, there ________.

6. What does the baby want?

   The baby ________.

Unit 7

My Body

VOCABULARY I

1 **Listen and check.** Then ask and answer. Point. Work with a partner. **TR: 7.1**

2 Look and write.

an arm	a hand
an ear	a head
an eye	a leg
feet	a mouth
a foot	a neck
hair	a nose

SONG

1 **Listen to the song.** Write. Use words from the box. **TR: 7.2**

clap	feet	hands	jump
legs	mouth	sing	walk

1. Legs, legs. Move your ___________.

   Can you ___________ with me?

2. Feet, feet. Move your ___________.

   Can you ___________ with me?

3. Mouth, mouth. Move your ___________.

   Can you ___________ with me?

4. Hands, hands. Move your ___________.

   Can you ___________ with me?

2 **Listen and draw.** Add labels. Use words from the box. **TR: 7.3**

body
feet
hands
legs
mouth

GRAMMAR I

Possessive adjectives

I	have	black	hair.	**My**	hair	is	black.
You				**Your**			
He	has			**His**			
She				**Her**			

1 Listen and read. Circle. TR: 7.4

1. My nose is small. Your nose is small.
2. My eyes are green. Her eyes are green.
3. Your hands are small. His hands are small.
4. Her mouth is red. His mouth is red.
5. Our hands are small. Their hands are small.

2 Listen and read. Circle. TR: 7.5

1. **Her / His** feet are small.
2. **His / My** feet are big.
3. **Her / His** hands are big.
4. **His / Her** hands are small.
5. Is **your / my** nose small?

3 **Look.** Write about the girl and her grandfather. Use words from the box.

Her	His

1. She is short.

   ________ legs are short.

   ________ arms are short.

2. He is tall.

   ________ feet are big.

   ________ hands are big.

3. Look at her head.

   ________ hair is black.

   ________ mouth is small.

   ________ nose is small.

4. Look at his head.

   ________ hair is white.

   ________ mouth is big.

   ________ nose is big.

4 **What about you?** Write about your head.

1. ______ hair is ________________________.

2. ______ mouth is ________________________.

3. ______ nose is ________________________.

4. ______ eyes are ________________________.

VOCABULARY 2

1 Look and read. Circle.

1. walk run

2. run jump

3. walk run

4. strong legs
   small legs

5. short neck
   long neck

6. strong arms
   short arms

2 Read and check. Then ask a partner.

	Me	My partner
strong legs		
long legs		
jump		
long hair		
walk		
strong hands		
run		

GRAMMAR 2

Ability with *can*

I	**can**	draw.
He/She		

Question			Answer	
Can	you	draw?	Yes,	I **can**.
	he/she			he/she **can**.

1 **Listen.** Write. **TR: 7.6**

1. No. He _______ walk.
2. _______ his sister jump?
3. Yes, she _______ run.
4. _______ the baby run?

2 **Look at the photos.** Read. Write.

1. Can the father cook?

_____, he __________________.

2. Can the brother clean?

_____, he __________________.

3. Can the baby sister cook?

_____, she __________________.

4. Can she watch TV?

_____, she __________________.

GAME TIME!

1 **Play a game.** Cut out the cards on page 119. Take a card. Read the question. Answer. Take turns.

2 **Read and match.** Write fun sentences.

Can you	walk	on the grass?
Can a baby	run	in the ocean?
Can a mother	jump	on one foot?
Can he	cook	on two feet?
Can she	sleep	in a river?
Can I	eat	in a kitchen?
		in a bedroom?

1. Can you cook in a kitchen?
2. ________________
3. ________________
4. ________________

3 **Read the questions in Activity 2.** Write answers.

1. ________________
2. ________________
3. ________________
4. ________________

READING

1 Listen and read. TR: 7.7

Polar Bears

These bears are polar bears. The small polar bears are babies. Their legs are short. Their mother is big. She has a big body. Her head is small. Her eyes and ears are small. Polar bears can walk and jump. Their legs are strong. A polar bear can stand on two legs!

2 Read. Circle.

1. A mother polar bear is **big. / small.**
2. Baby polar bears are **big. / small.**
3. Polar bears have strong **arms. / legs.**
4. A mother polar bear has a **big / small** head.
5. A mother polar bear has a **big / small** body.
6. Baby polar bears have **short / long** legs.

❸ **Look at the chart.** Read. Write.

Big Polar Bear

What does it have?
a big body
a small head
____
____
____

What can it do?
stand on two legs
____
____

❹ **Read and write.**

1. A big polar bear has a ______________ head.
2. It has ______________ legs.
3. A big polar bear can stand on ______________.

❺ **What about you?** What do you have? What doesn't a polar bear have? Write.

I have ______________________________.

A polar bear doesn't have ______________________________.

WRITING

1 **Draw a picture of yourself.** Write about your body. Use words from the box.

arms	ears	eyes	feet	foot	hair
hands	head	legs	mouth	neck	nose

My name is ______________________.

I have ______________________.

I have ______________________.

My ____________ is ____________.

My ____________ is ____________.

I have ______________________.

2 **Look and write.**

Who? What?	***has, have, is, are***
She	has short hair.
I	have long hair.
My hair	is brown.
Her hair	is black.
Her eyes	are green.

1. He ______ long legs.
2. Her legs ______ short.
3. My eyes ______ brown.
4. His nose ______ small.

UNIT 7 REVIEW

1 **Read.** Look at the picture. Circle.

1. He can jump.
2. His legs are long.
3. Its neck is long.
4. Its ears are long.
5. Her arms are strong.

2 **Look at the picture.** Read. Write.

1. Who can run? ____________________
2. Who can eat? ____________________
3. Who can sleep? ____________________
4. Who can jump? ____________________

Unit 8

Good Food

VOCABULARY I

1 **Listen and check.** Then ask and answer. Point. Work with a partner. **TR 8.1**

1. ______________

2. ______________

3. ______________

4. ____________ 5. ____________ 6. ____________

7. ____________ 8. ____________ 9. ____________

10. ____________ 11. ____________ 12. ____________

2 Look and write.

an apple	a cookie	rice
a banana	an egg	a salad
a cheese pizza	fish	a sandwich
chicken	an orange	soup

SONG

1 **Listen to the song.** Read. Draw lines to match. **TR: 8.2**

1. Pizza?

   I like pizza!

2. Apples?

   I like apples!

3. Chicken?

   I like chicken!

2 **Listen to the song.** Write. Use words from the box. **TR: 8.3**

Do you want a ________?

Do you want some ________?

Do you want a ________?

Yes, please!

banana	cheese	cookie

3 **Write a new verse for the song!** Use words from the box.

Do you want ____________________?

Do you want ____________________?

Do you want ____________________?

Yes, please!

an apple
some chicken
an egg
some fish
an orange
some rice
a salad

GRAMMAR I

like with count and noncount nouns

Question				Answer		
Do	you	**like**	eggs?	Yes, I **do**.	I **like** eggs.	*don't = do not*
				No, I **don't**.	I **don't like** eggs.	
Does	he		soup?	Yes, he **does**.	He **likes** soup.	*doesn't = does not*
				No, he **doesn't**.	He **doesn't like** soup.	

1 **Listen.** Write. TR: 8.4

1. Do you like salad?
2. Does she like fish?
3. ______ you ______ oranges?
4. ______ he ______ bananas?
5. ______ you ______ sandwiches?

2 **Listen.** Write. TR: 8.5

1. No, I don't. I don't like salad.
2. Yes, she does. She likes fish.
3. Yes, I ______. I ______ oranges.
4. No, he ______. He ______ bananas.
5. No, I ______. I ______ sandwiches.

3 **Read.** Check ✓ the foods you like. Make an ✗ for the foods you don't like. Then compare your answers with a partner.

	I like	I don't like	My partner likes	My partner doesn't like
bananas				
soup				
eggs				
apples				
rice				
fish				

4 **Look at the chart.** Write the foods you like ☺. Write the foods you don't like ☹.

☺ ______________________________

____

☹ ______________________________

____

VOCABULARY 2

1 **Look and read.** Color.

1. Color the lemonade yellow.
2. Color the tea brown.
3. Color the milk white.
4. Color the orange juice orange.
5. What does not have a color? ________

2 **Read.** Check ✓. Then compare your answers with a partner.

	I like	I don't like	My partner likes	My partner doesn't like
milk				
water				
orange juice				
tea				
lemonade				

3 **Look at the chart.** Write what you like.

I like ____________________.

GRAMMAR 2

Indefinite articles: *a, an*

a + consonant	banana, cookie, sandwich
an + vowel (a, e, i, o, u)	arm, eraser, orange

1 **Listen.** Write *an* or *a*. **TR: 8.6**

1. Do you have ______ crayon?
2. I have ______ old pen.
3. Does the fish have ______ ear?
4. Does the puppet have ______ mouth?

2 **Read.** Write *an* or *a*.

1. I am eating ______ apple.
2. She has ______ orange.
3. Do you have ______ banana?
4. No, I have ______ salad.
5. He is eating ______ cheese pizza.
6. I want ______ egg.
7. Do you want ______ cookie?
8. Does the fish have ______ eye?
9. Does the puppet have ______ neck?

GAME TIME!

1 **Look at the picture.** Read. Color.

1. Color the salad green.
2. Color the rice white.
3. Color the chicken yellow.
4. Color the cookies brown.
5. Color the apple red.
6. Color the oranges orange.

2 **Play a game.** Start at **A**. Listen. Go through the maze to the house. **TR: 8.7**

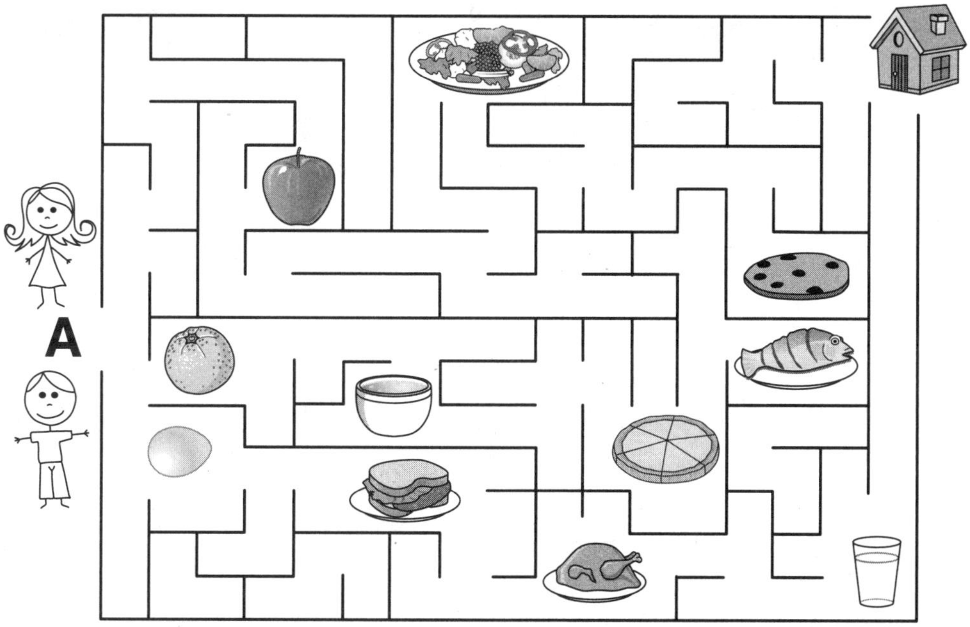

3 **Look.** What foods are in the maze?

____

____

READING

1 Listen and read. TR: 8.8

Fruit

Do you like fruit? Do you like juice? Do you like to eat fruit every day? What's your favorite fruit? What's your favorite juice?

Apples, oranges, and lemons are fruits. They grow on trees. Some fruit is from farms.

You can make juice from fruit. Use lemons and water to make lemonade. Apple juice, orange juice, and lemonade are delicious!

Use lemons and water to make lemonade.

a lemon

Lemons grow on trees.

2 Read. Circle yes or no.

1. Juice comes from fruit. yes no
2. Some people grow on trees. yes no
3. Apples grow on trees. yes no

3 **Look at the chart.** Read. Write.

Fruit

Where do people grow fruit?

____

What fruits grow on trees?

lemons

____

____

What can people do with fruit?

____

4 **Match.** Look. Read. Write the number.

1.

2.

3.

◯ This is an apple tree.

◯ These are orange trees.

◯ This is a lemon tree.

WRITING

1 **Look.** Write what the family likes to eat and drink.

1. The father likes ________________.
2. The mother likes ________________.
3. The girl is eating ________________.
4. Her brother is eating ________________.

2 **Read and write.**

Who?	What?
I/You	like pizza.
The girl	likes milk.
The boy	likes orange juice.

1. He ____.
2. She ____.
3. I ____.
4. You ____.

UNIT 8 REVIEW

1 **Look.** Read. Write.

1. What is the girl eating?

____

2. What does the boy have?

____

3. What is the grandmother eating?

____

4. What does the grandfather like?

____

5. Who likes tea?

____

2 **Listen.** Circle. TR: 8.9

1. Yes, I do. I like milk. — No, I don't. I like orange juice.
2. Yes, I do. I like water. — No, I don't. I don't like water.
3. Yes, I do. I like lemonade. — No, I don't. I like tea.

Unit 9

Animal Friends

VOCABULARY I

1 **Listen and check.** Then ask and answer. Point. Work with a partner. **TR: 9.1**

2 **Look and write.**

a cat	a donkey	a horse
a chicken	a duck	a rabbit
a cow	a frog	a sheep
a dog	a goat	a turtle

1. ____________________

2. ____________________

3. ____________________

4. ____________________

5. ____________________

6. ____________________

7. ____________________

8. ____________________

9. ____________________

10. ____________________

11. ____________________

12. ____________________

SONG

1 **Listen to the song.** Read. Write. Draw lines to match. **TR: 9.2**

1. I see one ______.

   Is it running?

   Yes, it's running.

2. I see two ______.

   Are they climbing?

   Yes, they're climbing.

3. I see three ______.

   Are they hopping?

   Yes, they're hopping.

hopping

running

climbing

2 **Write a new verse for the song!**

Use words from the boxes.

donkeys	eating	in the sun
goats	sleeping	on a mountain
rabbits	walking	on the grass

I see five ______________.

Are they ______________?

Yes, they're ______________.

They're ______________ ______________.

GRAMMAR I

Present progressive: *they are* + verb-*ing*

Question				Answer				
	Are	the goats	**running?**	Yes,	they	**are.**		*aren't = are not*
				No,	they	**aren't.**		
What	**are**	they	**doing?**		They'**re**		**eating.**	*They're = They are*

1 **Listen.** Write. TR: 9.3

1. What __are__ the cats doing?
2. What are the horses __doing__?
3. What are the goats ________?
4. What ________ the cows doing?
5. What are the sheep ________?

2 **Listen.** Write. TR: 9.4

1. __They're__ running.
2. They're __jumping__.
3. ________ eating.
4. They're ________.
5. ________ ________.

3 **Look at the picture.** Read. Write.

1. What are the frogs doing? They're jumping.
2. What are the ducks doing? ______________________
3. What are the donkeys doing? ______________________
4. What are the dogs doing? ______________________

4 **Look at the picture.** Read. Circle. Then check your answers with a partner.

1. Are the rabbits jumping? Yes, they are. No, they aren't.
2. Are the chickens running? Yes, they are. No, they aren't.
3. Are the cats eating? Yes, they are. No, they aren't.

VOCABULARY 2

1 **Look.** Read. Match. Write the numbers.

1. The goat is climbing.
2. The cat is crawling.
3. The sheep see a dog.
4. The ducks are swimming.
5. The ducks are flying.

2 **Listen.** Read. Write. TR: 9.5

1. I ____________ two turtles.
2. The turtles are ____________.
3. The chicken is ____________.
4. A girl is ____________.

GRAMMAR 2

want **+ infinitive**

<table>
<tr><th colspan="5">Question</th><th colspan="2">Answer</th></tr>
<tr><td rowspan="2">Do</td><td rowspan="2">you</td><td rowspan="4">want</td><td rowspan="4">to see</td><td rowspan="4">the cows?</td><td>Yes, I do.</td><td rowspan="2">don't = do not</td></tr>
<tr><td>No, I don't. I want to see the ducks.</td></tr>
<tr><td rowspan="2">Does</td><td rowspan="2">Ivan</td><td>Yes, he does.</td><td rowspan="2">doesn't = does not</td></tr>
<tr><td>No, he doesn't. He wants to ride the horse.</td></tr>
</table>

1 **Listen.** Write. TR: 9.6

1. __Do__ you __want to ride__ a horse?
2. What ______ you __________________?
3. ______ Lena __________________ the goats?
4. What ______ she __________________?
5. ______ you __________________ the chickens?

2 **Listen.** Circle. TR: 9.7

1. No, I don't. No, she doesn't.
2. I want to see the goats.
   She wants to see the goats.
3. No, I don't. No, she doesn't.
4. I want to ride the donkey.
   She wants to ride the donkey.
5. No, I don't. No, she doesn't.

GAME TIME!

1 **Look at the picture.** What are the animals doing? Read. Check ✓.

	birds	chickens	frogs	goats	rabbits
eating					
swimming					
flying					
sleeping					
climbing					

2 **Write questions.** Ask a partner. Write the answers.

Do you		six donkeys?
Does she	want to see	two horses?
Does he	want to ride	a bike?
Does a turtle		a goat?
Does a dog		three sheep?

1. *Do you want to see a goat?* ______ *Yes, I do.*
2. ______________________ ______________
3. ______________________ ______________
4. ______________________ ______________

READING

1 Listen and read. TR: 9.8

Pets

Many people have animals at home. They are called pets. Pets make people happy. Many people have a cat or a dog. Some people have other animals as pets. Goats are good pets. They like to play and jump! Turtles are fun pets, too. They like swimming.

People can have baby animals for pets. A baby cat is a kitten. A baby goat is a kid. A baby turtle is a hatchling. Some people have just one pet. Some people have many pets! People all over the world have pets.

2 Read. Circle yes or no.

1. Baby animals are not good pets. yes no
2. Baby goats are called kids. yes no
3. Many people have pets. yes no

3 Read and write.

1. What is a baby cat called? ______________
2. What do goats like to do? ______________
3. What is a baby turtle called? ______________

4 **What about you?** Work with a partner. Ask and answer.

1. Do you have a pet?

   I ______________________________.

2. What pets do you like?

   I like ______________________________.

WRITING

1 **Look at the picture.** The boy's name is Ivan. He has ducks. Color the ducks. Then write about them.

1. How many ducks does Ivan have?

   Ivan has ____________________.

2. What are their names?

   Their names are ____________________.

3. What colors are the ducks?

   They're ____________________.

4. What are the ducks doing?

   ____

   ____

2 **Circle the animal you want.** Color it.
Write about it.
What color is it?
What is it doing?

I want ____________________

____

____________________.

UNIT 9 REVIEW

1 **Look.** Read. Write.

1. What does the girl want to do?

   She ______________________________.

2. Does the boy want to see the sheep? ______________.

3. What does the boy want to do?

   He ______________________________.

4. What do the sheep want to do? They ______________.

2 **Play a game.** Cut out the cards on page 125. Play with a partner. Ask and answer.

Review: Units 7–9

1 Listen. Circle. TR: R3.1

1. Do you like sheep?   Does he like sheep?
2. Yes, I do. I like sheep.   No, I don't. I don't like sheep.
3. Yes, she does. She likes lemonade.   No, she doesn't. She likes milk.
4. I can climb. I have strong arms.   He can climb. He has strong arms.
5. The chicken can swim.   The chicken can fly.
6. I want to ride a donkey.   She wants to ride a donkey.

2 Write and match.

1. I see ___a___ cow.

2. I want to eat ________ egg.

3. Does ________ rabbit have long ears?

4. I want to eat ________ apple.

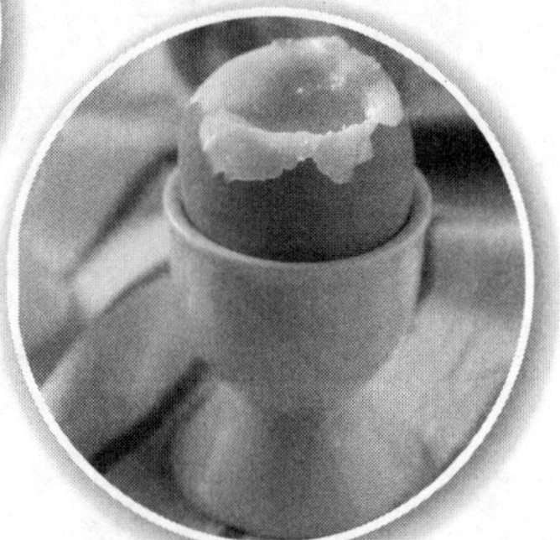

5. Does he want to eat ________ orange?

3 **Read.** Look at the picture. Circle.

1. The turtle has a long neck.
2. The goat likes sandwiches.
3. She likes salad.
4. Her hair is long. She has a sandwich.
5. His hand is on his ear. His foot is on the rock.

4 **Look at the picture.** Read. Circle.

1. What are the horses doing?

   They're walking.   They're running.

2. What is the frog doing?

   It's swimming.   It's jumping.

3. Are the goats sleeping?

   Yes, they are. They're sleeping.   No, they aren't. They're eating.

4. Are the ducks swimming?

   Yes, they are. They're swimming.   No, they aren't. They're flying.

Unit 1 Use with Activity 2 on page 11.

t	p	r	e	o	l
m	a	c	i	p	b
d	o	i	e	l	n
s	r	c	h	k	y

Unit 7 Use with Activity 1 on page 87.

Can you jump?	Can you run on the grass?	Can you walk on the moon?	Can you cook?	Can you watch TV?
Can you clean your bedroom?	Can you eat a cloud?	Can you sing?	Can you walk?	

Unit 5 Use with Activity I on page 61.

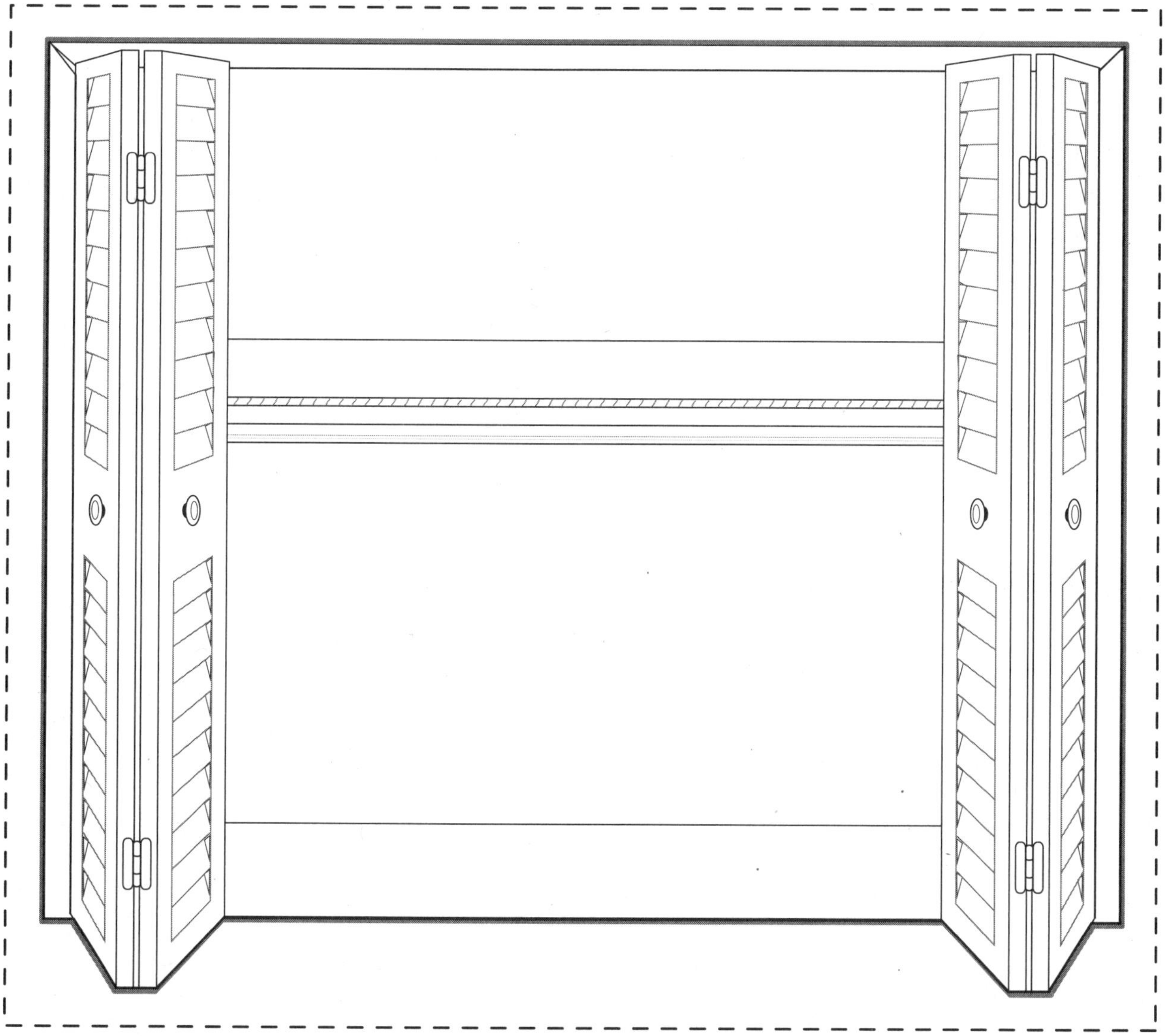

Unit 6 Use with Activity I on page 73.

a robot	a puppet	a drum	a truck
a ball	a drum	a bike	a puzzle
a puppet	a kite	a doll	a train

Unit 9 Use with Activity 2 on page 115.